M000166838

To

_____

From

_____

© 2000 by Bruce Bickel and Stan Jantz

ISBN 1-57748-887-3

Cover art: Debra Dixon

Published by Promise Press, an imprint of Barbour Publishing, Inc., P.O. Box 719, Uhrichsville, Ohio 44683 http://www.barbourbooks.com

Printed in China.

GOD IS IN THE
SMALL STUFF
for WOMEN

BRUCE & STAN

PROMISE
PRESS
An Imprint of Barbour Publishing

We encourage you to closely examine and cherish the seemingly everyday, ordinary circumstances of your life. Why? Because God is in the details of your life.

"*What* makes God so clear to us is not so much His big blessings to us, but the tiny things, because they show His amazing intimacy with us— He knows every detail of each of our individual lives."

OSWALD CHAMBERS

~

*Look! Here I stand
at the door and knock.
If you hear me calling
and open the door,
I will come in,
and we will share
a meal as friends.*

REVELATION 3:20 NLT

God makes Himself available, but you must respond to His invitation. Take Him at His Word. Go to Him. Open the door of your heart to Him. You don't have to call to schedule an appointment. He has already extended the invitation, and He's waiting for you to respond.

~

You begin to seek God for who He is when you stop seeking Him for what He can do for you.

~

Have a passion for God and compassion for people.

~

The only love that is completely other-centered is called *agape* love. It's what C. S. Lewis called "Divine Gift-Love." When we love with *agape* love we desire the best for the people we love. We are even able to love those who are unlovable.

~

Love is the essence of God. Love is what motivates Him to do what He does for us— down to the last detail—even when we don't love Him in return. Knowing that should give tremendous meaning to our lives.

We love God because we know
who He is. God loves us despite
who we are.

~

*God's unconditional
love for us
should motivate us
to love others
unconditionally.*

~

God wants you to grow spiritually because when you do, your life becomes more meaningful and more satisfying. Just like you feel when you make the consistent effort to improve physically, you will feel great about yourself when you make the effort to improve spiritually. And even better than that, the people around you will experience the benefits of your growth.

~

*A spiritually
mature individual
places more
importance on God's
internal presence
than on the world's
external signs.*

When you read the Bible, you are reading God's message for you. The Bible is not just an option for knowing God and the secrets of the universe. It's the *only* way for you to accurately discover the details of God's plan for you.

~

If you don't have a Bible, get one.
If you've got a Bible, read it.
If you read the Bible, believe it.
If you believe the Bible, live it.

If the Bible is God talking to us, then prayer is us talking to God. It's the primary way of connecting to the infinite, all-powerful, all-knowing, all-loving God. Without prayer you can never get close to God.

~

Don't pray for a lighter load.
Pray for a stronger back.

~

*Pray as if the task
depends on God
and work as if
it depends on you.*

~

One of the best ways to keep your life whole is to pay attention to the small stuff. Do what it takes every day to develop your character and preserve your integrity. Most of all don't live your life to please others. Live your life to please God.

~

If you want to know what's in
your heart, listen to your mouth.

~

Be honest
with yourself.
Be honest
with other people.
Be honest with God.

~

~

*If you're going
to compare yourself
to anyone,
compare yourself
to Jesus.
It will put your
life in perspective.*

~

Even though Jesus is a perfect moral example for us, it isn't enough. Because none of us is perfect. None of us can do what Jesus did *all* the time, in every detail of our lives. We need help. More than that, we need forgiveness when we sin. But who will help us? In a word, Jesus.

So when does your quest to improve yourself end? When you stop breathing. Between now and then, you should consider yourself to be an ongoing project. A work in progress. Always improving. Never stagnant.

Self-improvement doesn't happen automatically. It requires constant, systematic, and disciplined personal development. There are books to be read, people to meet, and new places to discover. Your personal growth is a privilege, not a burden. This is where God loves to get involved in the details of your life. Let Him in and watch Him work in the small stuff of your life to help you grow and improve.

We may be spiritual creatures at heart, but while we're on Earth our spirits are being housed in our physical bodies. Let's do everything we can to keep the house in top shape.

~

~

Fitness of the soul
should take priority
over fitness of
the body,
but the two
are not mutually
exclusive.

~

The reason our lives are so complicated is that we're too self-centered. Richard Foster writes that "simplicity means moving away from total absorption in ourselves. . .to being centered in. . .God"

~

When you trust God and let Him take the lead in your life, you will find that your life will be more peaceful and more productive. You will naturally want to clear out the clutter to make more room for God.

If you're an average person trying to get ahead in the world, contentment is probably the last thing you're striving for, yet there's a good chance that you long for it. Why? Because at its core, contentment is peace of mind. Contentment is happiness. The person who is content has little or no stress.

~

It's not only possible but desirable to be both content and ambitious. If your ambitions come from a desire to serve God, to help others, and to improve yourself so you will have a greater impact in your world, then the fulfillment of your ambitions will bring you much happiness and contentment.

~

*"It is not only wrong to worry,
it is unbelief;
worrying means we
do not believe that God can
look after the practical details
of our lives,
and it is never anything but
those details that worry us."*

OSWALD CHAMBERS

Clearly the antidote to worrying is trusting God to take care of the small stuff of your life. Invite Him to get involved in the details of your life. "Give all your worries and cares to God," says the Bible, "for he cares what happens to you" (1 PETER 5:7 NLT).

~

Anxiety is short-lived if we give it to God.

~

*Instead of worrying
about what
you can't do,
think about
what God can do
for you.*

~

*Dear brothers
and sisters,
whenever trouble
comes your way,
let it be an
opportunity for joy.
For when your
faith is tested,
your endurance has
a chance to grow.*

Is God calling you near in your time of trouble? Go to Him in prayer and through His Word. There you'll find strength, safety, and solace. Are you hurting? Do you struggle with loneliness? God wants you to draw near to Him so you can feel His overwhelming love. Go ahead. Ask God for His comfort in every detail of your life.

~

~

*Rather than
using God to solve
your problems,
use your problems
to get closer
to God.*

~

At the beginning of each year, choose a topic of interest and spend the next twelve months learning all you can about it.

If you take a little time a few times each week to jot down your thoughts, you will be amazed at the results. You will find that the small stuff in your life will feel more ordered, and the big stuff won't seem so imposing.

~

Whenever someone has done something nice for you, write a thank-you note. When someone needs a lift, write a personal note of encouragement. When tragedy strikes another, express your sympathy with a heartfelt card. You'll never know how meaningful your written words will be to others.

~

People seldom think of encouragement as a gift because it seems so ordinary. But it isn't.

Encouragement is actually quite rare (because it's seldom given) and it is valuable (because it's so meaningful to the recipient). In our humble opinion, encouragement makes the perfect gift, and here's why:

- It's free.
- It requires no shopping.
- It doesn't have to be gift-wrapped.
- It can be custom-designed.
- It doesn't require batteries.
- It will last a lifetime.

When it comes to generosity, ask yourself two questions. First, does your generosity come from your heart? A truly generous person gives out of love and compassion, not from a desire to impress others. Second, is your generosity productive? Remember, each time you give to those "in need," you are making an investment in God's resources. Invest wisely.

~

*Give the gift
of time.
It's a gift
more valuable
than money can buy.*

The generous person always has
more than enough; the greedy person never has enough.

Simply giving something—whether it's your money or your time—doesn't necessarily mean you have compassion for someone else. Never make the mistake of equating generosity with compassion. If anything, a generous spirit flows from your compassion, not the other way around. True compassion means that you see other people the way God sees them.

~

*Don't wait to
do one great thing
for God in your
lifetime.
Rather, do many
good little things
for the sake of
His kingdom,
which in itself
is a great thing.*

Make your home a place that is filled with laughter. That won't be difficult if you look for humor in the small stuff of life. Start with the family photo album. Laughter shared between parents and children is a guaranteed formula for producing well-adjusted children. A child who knows how to enjoy laughter is better equipped to handle life as an adult.

~

*If you can laugh
at yourself,
you are guaranteed
a lifetime
of chuckling.*

The truth is that we don't criticize others in order to help them. We criticize in order to make ourselves feel more important.  We end up exaggerating the faults of others while excusing or ignoring our own shortcomings.

Honest self-evaluation is really nothing more than letting God into the details of your life. When you do this you open yourself up to self-improvement. Here's what's going to happen: God will bring to your consciousness an awareness of areas where you need to improve; He will speak to you through His Word, and God will use people to give you honest (and sometimes painful) evaluations of your behavior.

~

There is one aspect of life which cannot be rushed—building a meaningful relationship with another person. You can make an acquaintance "on the spot," but a friendship won't happen instantaneously. And it doesn't develop overnight. It takes *time*. The most precious commodity of our "hurry up" society must be invested over the long-term if you expect to have a friendship that is dependable and fulfilling.

~

Growing a friendship is not unlike growing a crop.

There has to be a season of planting: Time is spent in finding common interests.

There has to be a season of growing: You begin to appreciate each other's differences.

There is a lifelong season of harvest: The friendship proves to be a source of strength and encouragement to you.

~

Being a friend is a choice. Here are four different types of friendships you could choose to be involved with. Choosing to establish these friendships will give you great fulfillment, and you will enrich the lives of others.

- Be a disciple.
- Be a mentor.
- Be accountable.
- Be a neighbor.

~

*A friend is
always loyal,
and a brother
is born to help
in time of need.*

PROVERBS 17:17 NLT

The one love that will keep your marriage together is *agape* love, which is the love that desires the best for the other person. This is unselfish love that seeks to give rather than take. This is love that takes work.

~

If loving your spouse unselfishly is a challenge for you, think about the way Jesus loves you. The Bible says that Jesus willingly "made himself nothing" in order to completely serve those He loved. And now He asks you to love your spouse in the same sacrificial way.

~

Your child's greatest need is the security of knowing that you care. There is no better way to convey your love than to spend time with your child. Hours invested in your child will produce dividends now and in the future. You will be building a relationship, moment by moment, that will be the basis for a lifelong friendship between the two of you.

~

Teach your chil- dren by your words (make sure they are kind), by your actions (make sure they are wholesome), and by your tem- perament (make sure it is controlled).

Do you want your child to learn the meaning of honesty? Then be honest yourself. Admit to making a mistake; acknowledge that you don't know all of the answers; and don't cover up your own shortcomings.

$\mathcal{D}o$ you want your teenager to have moral character? Then don't make promises unless you know you can keep them. Be just and equitable in establishing the rules of the household. Don't require any behavior from your child that you don't consistently exhibit yourself.

~

Once away from home, your child lives independently without any obligation of accountability to you. How do you convey your interest and concern without being accused of meddling? Here are a few suggestions:

- Keep checking in without checking up.
- Learn to listen instead of lecture.
- Give advice only when asked.
- Ask questions for the sake of praying, not prying.

The parents' role
is not to make
all the right choices
for their children,
but to teach them
how to make
those choices
for themselves.

Before He created the universe ages ago, God knew all about us. We should not be surprised that He has ordered our days and is interactively involved in the events of our daily routine. Nothing escapes His notice. Nothing is too insignificant for His care. Live your life with an overwhelming sense that God is present in the details all around you. There will be no boring moments. Life will take on a new meaning when you begin to see God in the small stuff.

When you know that God works through your circumstances, they will energize you. So go out and make a difference in your world. Leave an impression on everything and everyone you touch because of what God has done for you.

About the Authors

Bruce Bickel is a lawyer and **Stan Jantz** is a marketing consultant. But don't let those mundane occupations fool you. Bruce and Stan have collaborated on fifteen books, with combined sales of more than a million copies. Their passion is to present biblical truth in a clear, correct, and casual manner that encourages people to connect in a meaningful way with the living God.

Bruce and his wife, Cheryl, live in Fresno, California; they are active at Westmont College where Bruce is on the Board of Trustees and their two children attend. Stan and his wife, Karin, also live in Fresno; they are involved at Biola University where Stan is on the Board of Trustees and their two children attend.

Contact Bruce & Stan at: www.bruceandstan.com

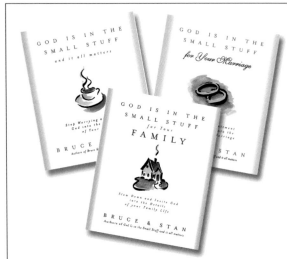

AVAILABLE WHEREVER BOOKS ARE SOLD

256 pages each; $12.99